5193

Antioch Community High School
Library
1133 S. Main Street
Antioch, IL 60002

DEMCO

Facing competition

WHAT DO YOU KNOW ABOUT COMPETITION? TAKE THIS QUIZ NOW—AND THEN AFTER YOU READ THIS BOOK, TAKE IT AGAIN, COMPARE YOUR ANSWERS, AND FIND OUT WHAT YOU'VE LEARNED! **True or False?**

1 If I don't play sports, I don't have to worry about competition.

2 Everyone knows that competition is necessary for people to succeed.

3 Setting goals is primarily an activity for adults who have professional careers.

4 Competition is damaging to people of all ages, especially children.

5 Social competition affects children, adolescents, teens, and adults.

6 Competing is a normal human instinct.

7 Very few people ever actually cheat in school, at work, or with sports.

8 Many people enjoy the challenge found in competition.

Answer key: (1) False; (2) False; (3) False; (4) False; (5) True; (6) False; (7) False; (8) True.

What does it mean to win or lose?

For my parents, Alice and Paul Stouffer

Photographs © 2007: age fotostock/Photodisc: 97; Al Oliver/Jason Jones Kicker Audio: 71 center; AP/Wide World Photos: 98 (Stefano Rellandini), 57; Corbis Images: 91 (Paul Barton), 100 (Bettmann), 2 (Randy Faris), 103 (Patrik Giardini), 16 (Grace/zefa), 55 (Andanson James/Sygma), 37 top (Hughes Martin), 9 (Colin McPherson), 34 (Richard Milner/epa), 39 (Roy Morsch), 24 (Michelle Pedone), 21 (Jose Luis Pelaez, Inc.), 11 (Lew Robertson), 6, 18, 53, 82, 93 (Royalty-Free), 71 left (Christina Salvador/Sygma), 65 (Eric K.K. Yu); Getty Images: 37 bottom (Alistair Berg), 26 (Chris Clinton), 17 (Nancy Honey), 5 bottom (Dorling Kindersley), 49 (Lori Adamski Peek), 84 (West Rock), 15 (Michael Smith), 69 (Rick Stewart); International Swimming Hall of Fame: 4, 10; JupiterImages/Image Source: 38; Landov, LLC: 71 right (Gary Hershorn/Reuters), 67 (George Ruhe/Bloomberg News); Monty Stilson: cover; Omni-Photo Communications/Paul Slaughter: 29; PhotoEdit/Michael Newman: 5 top, 62; photolibrary.com/Adams Gregg: 44; Superstock, Inc.: 42; The Image Works: 30 (Eastcott-Momatiuk), 23 (Nancy Richmond); yosemitestock. com/Chris Falkenstein: 12.

Cover design: Marie O'Neill
Book production: The Design Lab

Library of Congress Cataloging-in-Publication Data
Davidson, Tish.
  Facing competition : can you play by the rules and stay in the game? /
Tish Davidson. — 1st ed.
    p. cm. — (Choices)
  Includes bibliographical references and index.
  ISBN-10: 0-531-16754-2 (lib. bdg.)   0-531-16723-2 (pbk.)
  ISBN-13: 978-0-531-16754-0 (lib.bdg.)   978-0-531-16723-6 (pbk.)
  1. Competition (Psychology)—Juvenile literature. I. Title. II.
Series: Choices (Franklin Watts, Inc.)
  BF637.C47D38 2005
  302'.14—dc22
2004018605

1 2 3 4 5 6 7 8 9 10 R 16 15 14 13 12 11 10 09 08 07

SCHOLASTIC
CHOICES

Can you play
by the rules
and stay in
the game?

Facing

competition

Tish Davidson

Franklin Watts®

A DIVISION OF SCHOLASTIC INC.
NEW YORK • TORONTO • LONDON • AUCKLAND • SYDNEY
MEXICO CITY • NEW DELHI • HONG KONG
DANBURY, CONNECTICUT

table of contents

chapter one

6 Beauty and the Beast:
THE MANY MASKS OF COMPETITION
You compete every single day of your life for something: first turn in the bathroom, best seat on the bus, better grades, faster times, the best date for this Saturday. Competition is a part of life. Just beware of the different masks it can wear.

chapter two

24 I Win!
LEARNING TO COMPETE
Is competition just instinct? Is it something you learned somewhere along the way? Can societies actually survive in today's world without competition?

chapter three

42 But It Is GOOD for You!
THE PERKS OF COMPETITION
There are some definitely great things about competition. Whether it comes from inside or out, whether it's found at school, on the field, or in the marketplace, working to win can be good for you. Find out why.

chapter four

62 Too Much of a Good Thing? TAKING COMPETITION TOO FAR

Taking anything too far is never a good idea, and that is true with competition, too. What happens when you go to the extreme? What can the examples of others teach you? Find out here.

chapter five

82 Make It Work for You! KEEPING COMPETITION POSITIVE

Learning about competition doesn't do any good if you don't apply it to your own life. How can you make sure you capitalize on the positives and avoid the negatives? Here's how.

MORE INFORMATION

104 **Glossary**; 106 **Further Resources**;
108 **Index**; 112 **About the Author**

beauty
and the
beast

"I'VE LEARNED TO FIGHT FOR WHAT I WANT. NEVER GIVE UP."

The Many Masks of Competition

- "Competition gives me motivation to work harder and reach my potential."
- "It brings out the worst in me!"
- "I feel good when I win. It makes my parents proud."
- "Competition is exciting."
- "It's bad when you lose . . . really bad."
- "It stresses me out."

There is no question about it: competition wears different masks. While some of them may make you feel beautiful, others may make you feel more like a beast.

What do you think of when you think of competition? Does it make you think of achieving goals that you never thought were possible? Or does it create the idea of so much pressure that you just want to quit trying? It is different with each person.

Winning. Losing. Meeting goals. Making progress. Let's face it: competition is tough. It can make a group of individuals bond into a team—or it can ruin friendships. It has benefits. It has drawbacks. The one thing almost everyone can agree on, however, is this:

COMPETITION
is COMPLICATED!

"There is nothing noble in being superior to your fellow men. True nobility lies in being superior to your former self."

Elijah Wood

Competition has many faces and shapes. It can be **external**—where one person, team, or group wins and everyone else loses. It can also be **internal**—competing with yourself to reach new goals. It can even be social—a blending of both internal and external competition.

Competition is more than running a race, taking a test, or applying for a job. It is a basic part of American life. You are involved in competition every minute, from deciding whether to buy that shirt or see that movie to selecting what brand of soda to drink. It is little wonder you and other people have such strong feelings about competition. You experience it every single day.

A Close Call

Tim McKee churned through the water, pushing himself as hard as he ever had on the last lap of the 400-meter individual medley at the 1972 Olympics in Munich, Germany. The fourth of nine children in a competitive swimming family from Philadelphia, McKee had overcome mononucleosis to win a spot on the U.S. team.

Now it looked like he was headed for a gold medal as he hit the touch pad at the end of the lane. On the scoreboard next to his name was 4:31:98 and a number one, for first place.

There was a problem, however. In another lane, Gunnar Larsson of Sweden also had 4:31:98 and a number one. A tie? For eight minutes, the judges debated. The new electronic touch pads were able to separate swimmers by one-thousandth of a second. After looking at the computer tape, the judges declared Larsson the winner by two-thousandths of a second.

The difference between winning and losing the gold was about ten times shorter than the time it takes to blink!

You have seen people participate in international competitions like the Olympics. Contests to determine one person's or team's ability in comparison to others go on throughout the world in sports, education, and business. One person runs fastest. One student wins the spelling bee. One team wins the hockey league championship. One brand of car outsells all the others. An art collector bids highest at an auction to get the coveted painting. When there can be limited numbers of winners and everyone else is a loser, you have external competition.

Oh, My Aching Stomach!

Guinness World Records recently dropped forty-three records from its latest edition for health reasons. Among them, it omitted:

• **Alan Peterson's record for eating 20 hamburgers in 39 minutes.**
• **Peter Dowdeswell's record for eating 144 prunes in 35 seconds.**

France's Michel Lotito's record will stand. He has eaten seven bicycles, a supermarket cart, seven television sets, and an airplane— but not all in one sitting.

Climb to
SUCCESS

Mark Wellman began climbing mountains when he was 12. In 1982, while he was working as a ranger at Yosemite National Park, he fell while descending from a climb. He was paralyzed from the waist down. People assumed he'd never climb again.

They were wrong.

Instead, Wellman set a goal. Even though he could not use his legs, he would climb Yosemite's difficult El Capitan. Seven years of training later, he achieved his goal. It took him more than a week and seven thousand pull-ups to conquer the mountain's sheer granite cliffs. "Success depends upon the ability to face whatever challenges come our way," he said.

Competition within ourselves is called internal or personal competition. It is independent of doing better than another person. The challenge here is to reach a particular goal or level of achievement. Not every goal is as dramatic as Wellman's, of course. A student might set a goal of changing a class grade from a C to a B. A runner might want to complete a marathon or improve his or her personal best time. A strong swimmer might work to pass the American Red Cross lifeguard certification test. These are all called **process goals**. They focus on improving mastery of a skill rather than defeating another person. The skills gained through process goals can equip a person to achieve an even greater goal.

REMEMBER

THERE IS
NO LIMIT
TO WHAT YOU CAN ACHIEVE.

A Comparison of

EXTERNAL & internal

Competition

Internal Competition

It encourages personal growth and skill development.

Individuals set the goals.

Goals vary from person to person.

The goal is to improve a skill or reach a certain standard.

Any number of people can meet their goals.

Competitors work against themselves.

Success is measured by improvement.

Any pressure comes from the individual, not from others.

The reward is personal satisfaction.

External Competition

It creates public pressure to win from parents or fans.

It creates a group identified as losers.

There are rewards for the winners.

Goals are determined by rules.

Everyone competing has the same goal.

The only goal is to do better than others.

One person, team, or group wins.

Competitors work against each other.

It encourages doing just enough to win.

"The healthiest competition occurs when average people win by putting [forth] above-average effort."

Colin Powell

Variety

Ten girls ruled the social scene at Andrea's high school. They were the ones who decided which clothes were in and which ones were NOT. They made it clear which boys were hot—and not—and only paired up with the hottest ones.

Andrea admired the girls for their confidence and power and wanted to be one of them. When Terrence, one of the hot boys, asked her to the winter dance, she started ignoring

her friends. She started hanging out on the fringes of the popular girls' clique. She tried to get them to like her by telling exaggerated and embarrassing stories about her old friends. She even started a rumor about her former best friend just to make herself look better.

The popular girls tolerated Andrea while she was with Terrence, but when he dropped her after the dance, so did they. They began telling embarrassing stories about her. Andrea was hurt and upset. When she tried to go back to her old friends, they were mad at her. Now she was alone.

For many students, social competition is the type of competition that is most familiar. It is both internal and external: internal because one person sets the goal of becoming part of a specific social group, and external because it involves doing things or playing by unwritten "rules" in order to be accepted. Decisions about who is in and who is out are usually made by a small group, and the rules may involve wearing the "right" clothes, associating with the "right" people, playing the "right" sports, or other constantly changing status symbols. In high school, social competition can be vicious and irrational, especially when kids compete using rumors and gossip.

It doesn't end with high school!

Social competition can carry over into adult life. Adults often strive to:

- own the "right" car;
- live in the "right" neighborhood;
- know the "right" people;
- have the "right" job.

Competition is here to stay. It has the ability to improve—or harm—your body and your mind's well-being. Which role does it play in your life?

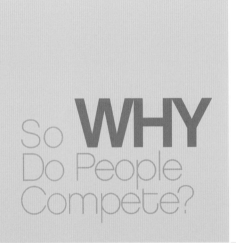

So **WHY** Do People Compete?

Constructive Reasons	Destructive Reasons
for fun and excitement	to please parents or other adults
to test their abilities	to win public recognition
to reach a higher goal	to gain social status
to feel good about succeeding	to avoid being left behind
as an outlet for emotions	to put down other people
to be part of a team	to keep other people at a distance

Just How COMPETITIVE Are YOU?

Do you think of yourself as a competitive person? Take this quiz and count the number of times you answer yes to see how competitive you really are.

(1) It's pizza day in the school cafeteria. Do you rush to the head of the line to get the best slice?

(2) Have you ever dated someone just because you knew it would make you more popular and not because you liked him or her?

(3) You are beating your younger sibling at your favorite video game. Do you do a victory cheer even though you suspect there are tears in your brother's or sister's eyes?

(4) You and your closest friend are up for the exact same job. Do you tell your potential new boss about your friend's habit of being late so you have a better chance of getting the job?

(5) Is there one person in your life that you have to always do better than?

(6) Will you check to see how other people did on this quiz to make sure you did better than they did?

Answer Key:

How many times did you answer yes?

0 Wow! You really don't have a competitive nature. You're chillin'.

1 That's pretty natural. Some level of competition is healthy.

2 You are mildly competitive. You are aware of its role in your life.

3 You are definitely leaning to the more competitive side.

4 You are quite competitive. It has an important place in your life.

5 You are very competitive. It is a high value to you.

6 You are extremely competitive, and others need to watch out!

THOUGHTS
to remember

Even some highly successful people disagree about how much competition is good for you!

Henry J. Kaiser, an American industrialist who became known as the father of modern American shipbuilding, said, "Live daringly, boldly, fearlessly. Taste the relish to be found in competition—in having put forth the best within you."

On the other hand, John D. Rockefeller, an industrialist who founded the Standard Oil Company, said, "Competition is a sin!"

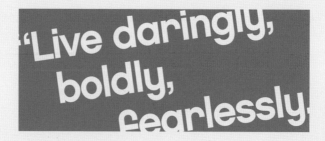
"Live daringly, boldly, fearlessly."

Use this book to:

1. Become aware of how competition is a normal part of your life.
2. Learn how it can be both GOOD and BAD for you.
3. Find out how to make competition work for you!

chapter two

George, 12

I win!

I win!

HE HAD HEARD IT ALL BEFORE AND IT NEVER MADE A DIFFERENCE.

Learning to Compete

George's father stopped the car in front of the school. Just before George opened the door, his dad said what he said every morning: "George, be the best in all your classes today."

George sighed.

He knew his father meant well, but there was no way he could be the best in every subject. That required more than just trying his hardest. It meant competing with everyone else in his class. Even at the age of 12, he knew that was impossible.

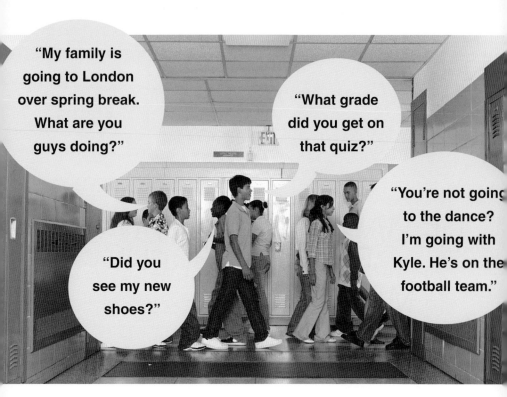

Competition is everywhere. Walk down any school hallway and you will hear kids jockeying for position. From making the team or wearing the current hot brand of clothing to getting superior grades or taking a high-status vacation, you are tuned in to the fine distinctions of who's on top, who wants to be, and who is at the very bottom. Whether the pressure to compete comes from trying to prove something to yourself or from wanting to please others, you live in a world where you are constantly being judged and judging others.

Plants and animals compete **instinctively** in their natural environments, but what about humans? Many people live in situations where they do not need to struggle for food, water, or shelter. Yet even when their survival needs are met, people spend huge amounts of time and energy trying to win contests of speed, strength, ability, academic achievement, and social or financial status.

COMPETITION BIG& small

At the simplest biological level, every living thing competes. From the tiniest bacterium in a pond fighting for its share of sunlight to the three-hundred-thousand-pound blue whale that needs eight thousand pounds of food every day, living things are in competition for the basics that allow them to stay alive—food, water, and shelter. Getting more of these resources allows plants and animals to fulfill their biological purposes and reproduce more successfully.

Instinct versus Learned Behavior

The drive to measure yourself against others is so much a part of our culture that many people think of it as a basic instinct. Americans, especially, believe in the value of competing to make more money and to make progress in sports, science, the arts, and industry. But what about people in other cultures?

"Is it POSSIBLE to live without competition?"

Social scientists have studied about two dozen cultures where competition—at least as we know it—does not exist. Their customs and beliefs strongly discourage comparisons of individual achievement, while encouraging mutual help, shared work, and shared responsibility for the welfare of the entire group.

Some of the better known noncompetitive societies are:
- the Inuit (native people of the Arctic)
- the !Kung (Bushmen of southern Africa)
- the Lepchas (Tibetan Buddhists in northern India)
- the Paliyan (a tribe in southern India)
- the Tahitians (native Pacific Islanders)

Cultures that reject competition raise their children to believe that no person is superior to or better than anyone else. They make sure that the well-being of each person is linked to the welfare of the entire group, and that every person feels secure in and dependent on the community. They look down on or exclude people who try to stand out above others or who refuse to share, and they usually connect their values to religious practices and rituals.

Most noncompetitive groups live in isolated areas, where they are shielded from many of the pressures and values of modern life. However, two groups that successfully reject competition can be found in the midst of one of the most competitive, achievement-oriented, individualistic countries in the world—the United States. The fact that these communities are able to maintain their competition-free lifestyles in the twenty-first century shows how learned social values can overcome any instinctive need to compete.

THE AMISH

The Amish are a Protestant religious group that came to the United States from Switzerland starting in 1717. While the majority live in Pennsylvania, smaller groups are in the Midwest and Canada. The Amish are known for their simple lifestyle and rejection of modern technology. They drive horse-drawn buggies rather than cars and live in houses without electricity or modern plumbing. Most Amish are farmers, although some are carpenters or craftsmen.

For four hundred years, the Amish have focused on work, worship, family, and community. Cooperation and conformity are emphasized over individual achievement. Their society is almost free of competition, aggression, and violence.

Amish children are taught at privately run schools. Education ends after eighth grade. Students are taught in one-room schoolhouses where twenty-five to forty children of all ages learn together in a supportive, noncompetitive environment. They are expected to do well, but there is no special recognition for doing exceptionally well.

The teacher instructs the oldest students, who, in turn, teach the younger ones. The emphasis is on learning accurately and thoroughly, rather than quickly. The goal is for all students to improve each day, regardless of their abilities. They are not ranked or compared, which encourages cooperation and discourages pride. Although there is virtually no competitive behavior in school, Amish-educated children often do better on standardized tests than their public school counterparts.

THE HUTTERITES

The Hutterian Brethren are a German-speaking Christian group that began in Europe In the 1500s. They came to the United States to avoid religious persecution. Communities can be found in the north-central part of the United States and in Canada.

For four hundred years, they have lived in colonies of 60 to 160 people. Property, except the most personal items, is owned by the community and shared as needed. Work is assigned based on ability, and income is shared equally. Like the Amish, Hutterites center their daily lives on work, worship, and community; however, they use modern technology in farming and manufacturing.

From birth, Hutterite children are exposed to communal living, encouraging sharing and collaborative work. Members of the community eat together in a common dining hall, worship together, and enjoy group recreation in their leisure time. Families are large, and multiple adults provide child care to all.

Even politics are noncompetitive. Leaders are nominated by community members but selected by lottery, so there is no campaigning. Taking pride in individual abilities is frowned upon, and the result is a peaceful, crime-free, cooperative society that has rejected competition for almost five centuries.

Charles Darwin

Social Darwinism

Charles Darwin (1809–1882), an English biologist who studied plants and animals, concluded that species change because of competition for natural resources. When a particular **trait** gives a plant or animal an advantage over its neighbors, that characteristic is more likely to be passed on to the next generation.

Herbert Spencer (1820–1903), a British sociologist, believed that Darwin's ideas could be applied to classes and races of people. He coined the phrase "survival of the fittest." By this, he meant it was a natural law that the best or "fittest" individuals controlled most of the resources and survived to become rich and successful, and they passed those abilities on to their children. The poor were poor because they were inferior and could not compete, according to Spencer. He wrote, "If they [the lower classes] are not sufficiently complete to live, they die, and it is best they should die."

This harsh philosophy was called Social Darwinism. It never caught on in England, but became popular in the United States. Businessmen in the late 1800s used this "natural law" as an excuse to make huge profits at the expense of their workers' health and well-being and to justify discrimination against the poor and racial minorities. In their minds, greed was good, because it encouraged competition that would rid society of weaker individuals and make the country stronger.

Although Spencer's ideas are now considered outdated and offensive, his influence remains. American society still sees competition, individual achievement, and the accumulation of wealth and power as positive social values.

Five-year-old Jason plays alone in his backyard. Over and over he tosses a ball into the air and tries to smack it with his bat. When he connects, he drops the bat and races around an imaginary base path, raising his arms in triumph when he crosses his pretend home plate. Jason is a typical preschooler. All he cares about is hitting the ball. He does not have to beat anyone or keep score to feel satisfied. Later, when he can reliably connect with the ball, he might make a game of trying to hit it farther and farther.

"This time, I ran a mile and I didn't have to stop and walk."

Researchers have found that unless adults emphasize winning, losing, and keeping score, children up to the age of 9 or 10 think of success in sports in terms of mastering a skill. When asked how they performed, they will say things like, "I practiced and practiced, and I finally scored a goal" or "This time, I ran a mile and I didn't have to stop and walk" or "My parents saw me do a really good dive!" Somewhere between the ages of 10 and 12, children begin to compare their performance to others.

"My parents saw me do a really good dive!"

"I practiced and practiced,
and I finally scored a goal."

What Did You Learn about
LEARNING TO COMPETE?

TRUE or FALSE?

(1) All societies in the world have some element of competition. It is a natural part of daily life.

(2) Charles Darwin was the sociologist who invented the concept of "the survival of the fittest."

(3) In your daily life, there are many examples of people judging you and you judging others.

(4) Reproducing successfully is the primary biological purpose of most living creatures.

(5) Most people recognize that competition is a learned behavior, not an instinct.

(6) Some cultures frown on celebrating individual achievements and talents.

(7) There are noncompetitive groups that coexist with traditional society and maintain their lifestyles.

(8) Most of the Amish can be found in Switzerland and Canada.

(9) Kids begin to compare their performances to others at about age 5 or 6.

(10) Men and women compete differently most of the time.

(1) **False. Remember the example of the Amish and the Hutterites? Those are just two of the cultures that have managed to eliminate competition from their lifestyles.**

(2) **False. That was Herbert Spencer. Darwin was a biologist.**

(3) **True. You may not be aware of it, but it is happening all the time.**

(4) **True. Humans are a little bit more complicated, but it is pretty true for them, too.**

(5) **False. Most humans consider the drive to compete a basic human instinct.**

(6) **True. In noncompetitive cultures, this is a basic tenet of their beliefs.**

(7) **True. The Amish and Hutterites are both clearly able to do this.**

(8) **False. They came from Switzerland, and now most are in Pennsylvania, the Midwest, and Canada.**

(9) **False. It usually starts when they are between 10 and 12.**

(10) **True. Males and females often have different attitudes about competition.**

chapter three

Reed, 16

but it is
GOOD
for you!

REED DID NOT LIKE LOSING TO ANYONE

The Perks of Competition

Nels and Reed had been friends since the third grade. They were both on their school's track team. Nels was their fastest distance runner. Reed could keep up until the last quarter mile, but then Nels would power ahead. At the beginning of the season, this happened in every race. Reed hated it. Even though their team was undefeated, Reed did not like losing to anyone. He began to train harder, working with his coach to build speed and stamina. His times improved, but so did Nels's.

It was the last meet of the year. As usual, Reed and Nels paced each other for most of the race. But this time, when they got to the spot where Nels usually pulled away, Reed kept up with him . . . and then he edged out in front. The finish line flashed by. Reed won, and both boys beat their personal best times.

Competition can be a great motivator. Although Reed and Nels were friends, the desire to win pushed both them to work harder and run faster. They both gained from the rivalry, and so did their team. Reed felt great about finally winning, and although Nels did not like losing the race, he was satisfied that he had

improved his personal best time. The rest of the team was proud that their teammates had finished in first and second places.

Going Inside!

Internal competition is what drives self-improvement and mastering skills. Can Marcus make ten free throws in a row without missing? He tries. He makes seven, then misses. He tries again. He misses after three. He tries again and makes nine and then . . . finally . . . ten. By the time he reached his goal of ten baskets without a miss, Marcus had done almost one hundred free throws. He could have simply practiced free throws, but he had more fun, got more satisfaction, and was more persistent because he had set a specific goal for himself.

With internal competition, you set your own goals. It gives you a way to measure your progress, independent of winning or losing.

Susan began riding horses when she was only 9 years old. Soon she was competing at schooling horse shows, the lowest level of competitive equestrian events. In one show, she won every class she entered. The following year, she moved up to the A-level circuit. Only occasionally would she win a ribbon, but when she did, she felt prouder and more satisfied than when she had won every class.

"My friends at school can't understand why I am so thrilled to come home with fourth or fifth place, but I know that I am competing against some of the best riders in the state and that I'm riding better now than I was when I was winning everything at lower level shows," she explains.

Looking Outside!

Stuart Walker, a physician and member of the 1968 United States Olympic team, has said that competition at its best is a performing art. This may sound extreme, but many people thrive on controlled, structured, external competition because it allows them to demonstrate in public the skills they have worked hard to acquire. Although winning is the goal, doing something well and doing it with a group of people who appreciate the effort involved feels great.

COMPETING develops **SELF-CONTROL**

RECOGNITION builds **SELF-ESTEEM**

With external competition, your opponent gives you a target to beat. This encourages you to work hard at becoming physically and mentally fit. Having a target pushes most people to do their best, as long as they and their opponents are somewhat evenly matched. As one tennis coach advised, "Try to find a practice partner who is a little better than you are. You won't always win, but you will improve." Working hard to beat an opponent adds to the satisfaction of winning.

External competition also allows you to practice taking calculated risks and making decisions. Shoot the ball or pass it? Go out in front in a race, or hang back and save yourself for the finish? Join the study group, or learn the material on your own? You must make decisions based on what you know about yourself, including your following characteristics:

- **traits**
- **preferences**
- **personality**
- **styles**
- **history**
- **strengths**
- **weaknesses**

Learning to evaluate risk is an important skill. External competition gives you the chance to practice risk-taking in a safe, structured environment. It also meets the need for excitement. "I don't have to drive a car down the highway at 90 miles per hour," says Susan, the horseback rider. "I get enough of an adrenaline rush jumping my horse over a four-foot fence at a horse show."

Lastly, external competition helps you learn self-control and how to cope with losing. Not every competition turns out as well for everyone as the race between Nels and Reed. When you lose, it is easy to be bitter and angry, especially if you feel you have performed well.

"It's hard to look at the other team celebrate when you feel you deserved to win more than they did," said Jamison Data, a high school soccer player from Fremont, California. According to Data, his team lost a hard-fought sectional championship despite superior play. No one wins every time, and not every loss will seem fair. Learning to accept defeat without lashing out and belittling your opponents, teammates, or the judges is a mark of maturity.

No one wins every time, and not every loss will seem fair.

Out in the Real World—An Example of Competition in the Marketplace

Just as external competition among individuals pushes them to work harder, achieve more, and do their best, competition among companies pushes them to pay more attention to their customers, find more efficient and less expensive ways of doing business, and create innovative products quickly. Before 1984, American Telephone and Telegraph (AT&T) was the only major telecommunications company in the United States. It was a monopoly.

MONOPOLY

when one company controls almost all of a product or service and can set the price, quality, or quantity of that product or service because there is no competition

In 1984, there were only a few styles and colors of telephones, and they had to be purchased from AT&T. All telephone service operated over AT&T landlines, and it was illegal to use non-approved telephones or answering machines on AT&T lines.

After a long court case, AT&T was split into seven regional telecommunication companies. The goal was to create competition. As a result, customers today have a choice of land-based lines, cellular phones, and even telephone connections over the Internet. There are hundreds of models and colors of regular phones, cordless phones, and cellular phones made by many different companies and selling for a wide range of prices. There are dozens of different calling plans offering combinations of local and long distance service, along with features such as voice mail, caller ID, and call blocking and forwarding.

The revolution in telephone service shows much of what is best about competition in the marketplace. Choices increased and prices dropped. New companies were formed. To stay in business, older companies had to develop new or improved products. The race to be first to provide innovative products and services quickly brought more choices to consumers. Quality was maintained or improved, since dissatisfied customers could easily switch to another company's products. People were no longer stuck with a service that might not meet their needs. Without competition, there would have been little incentive to move quickly to develop new technologies.

Competition in the marketplace lead to:

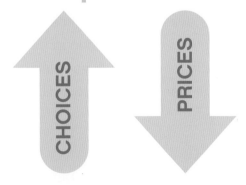

CHOICES

PRICES

The TEAMWORK is good and we act in unison. In keeping with our slightly different personalities, we share the tasks.

—Michel Platini (left), French soccer midfielder

Team Competition

In 1980, the United States Olympic ice hockey team was made up of talented college players, but no one gave them any chance of beating the powerful, disciplined, professional-style team of the Union of Soviet Socialist Republics (USSR).

Yet the unthinkable happened.

The players pulled together, working harder and playing better as a team than they ever had before. As a team, they rose above their individual skill levels and beat the Soviets 4–3. They then won the gold medal by defeating Finland 4–2.

TEAM	SCORE
USA	4
USSR	3

Team activities present a special set of competitive circumstances. Within the team, the goal is collaboration. Externally, the goal is to defeat an opponent. Ideally, there will be little conflict among team members because everyone is working toward the same external goal.

Teamwork helps people learn to communicate. Each team member must know what the others are doing in order to do his or her part. All jobs or positions on the team are important if the team is to succeed. By working together to defeat an opponent, strong bonds of respect and friendship often develop among team members. In school, teamwork is good practice for the business world, where employees often work in teams to beat the competition.

"The **STRENGTH** of **the team is each individual member . . . the strength of each member is the team.**"
—Coach Phil Jackson, Chicago Bulls

It Takes More Than Jerseys to MAKE A TEAM!

friendship

respect

cooperation

commitment

organization

TEAM

responsibility

collaboration

participation

communication

common goals

INSIDE OUT? OUTSIDE IN?

What Do You Know about External and Internal Competition Now?

On a separate piece of paper, write down what belongs in the blanks. Select answers from the choices in the box.

business	yourself	self-esteem
motivate	risks	weaknesses
goal	mastery	opponent
marketplace	strengths	

1. Competition works to _____ people.

2. With internal competition, you are competing against _____ .

3. Reaching any goal involves figuring out your _____ and _____ .

4. The primary goal of internal competition is _____ of a skill.

5. When others notice and recognize your achievements, it increases your _____ .

6. In external competition, you are traditionally going up against a(n) _____ .

7. One of the benefits of external competition is taking safe _____ .

8. One of the main places you see competition is in the _____ .

9. Teams work best if they all work toward a common _____ .

10. Teamwork helps prepare you for working in the world of _____ .

too much of a good thing

too much of a good thing

COMPETITION CAN TAKE THE JOY OUT OF AN ACTIVITY

Taking Competition Too Far

Can competition inspire people to work harder, longer, and smarter? Can it motivate individuals to set goals and improve their self-esteem? Absolutely.

Can it also push individuals to take unreasonable risks, bend or break the rules, and equate their self-worth with winning? You bet.

Competition can take the joy out of an activity, interfere with friendships, and encourage a win-at-any-costs mentality.

Doing well in school was very important to Elizabeth. She studied hard and was a straight-A student. In her junior year in high school, she enrolled in an honors physics class. The work was difficult and confusing. Soon Elizabeth was spending several hours a night just on homework for that class. In order to keep up in the rest of her subjects, she dropped out of all her extracurricular activities.

Sitting in the classroom, she was exhausted and nervous. At the end of the first semester, Elizabeth received the A she so desperately wanted in physics. During second semester, she surprised her friends by dropping the class. She said that she would rather drop it than risk "messing up."

if SELF-WORTH equals GOOD GRADES then EXPECTATIONS lead to PRESSURE

Elizabeth wanted to be a straight-A student. Trying to do well in school is a great goal, but in Elizabeth's case, she let it take over her life. She began defining her self-worth only by grades, not by what she learned, was good at, or enjoyed. In the end, her own expectations created so much pressure that she quit rather than risk not being perfect.

Any goal carried to extremes can have destructive physical or psychological effects. Take the case of Jenn. She was a slightly overweight 14-year-old. Her parents were proud of her when she began losing weight. But getting slimmer was not enough. Jenn wanted to be the thinnest person in her entire class.

She put herself on an extraordinarily strict diet. After losing forty pounds, she looked ill. In fact, she was ill. She was admitted to the hospital with a diagnosis of malnutrition and the eating disorder **anorexia nervosa**.

The pressure to get straight As and to lose weight came from inside Elizabeth and Jenn. They set their own goals and were not directly competing against another person. Instead, they were competing against an ideal image they had created of themselves. Their goals were too extreme. In the end, each girl's self-esteem and sense of value as an individual became tied to reaching completely unrealistic goals.

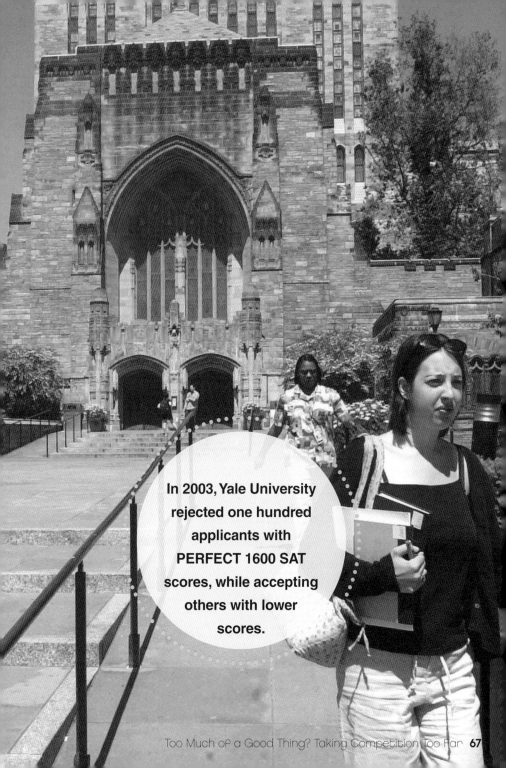

In 2003, Yale University rejected one hundred applicants with **PERFECT 1600 SAT** scores, while accepting others with lower scores.

It's Getting Complicated

Perhaps you are one of the one million high school basketball players who plan to play ball in college and then move on to the pros. If you are, you are not alone. In one study, 52 percent of black college basketball players said that they believed they would play in the NBA.

The reality?

Only 2.5 percent were drafted and played for at least one year.

DYING to Win?

Almost two hundred U.S. Olympic-caliber athletes were asked if they would take an undetectable banned drug that guaranteed them an undefeated record but would kill them in five years. More than HALF of them said YES, they would.

OUR CULTURE ELEVATES WINNING ATHLETES TO THE STATUS OF HEROES.

The high visibility of professional athletes—many of whom came from humble backgrounds and have acquired money, power, and glamour through their ability to play sports—has encouraged students and their parents to believe that being a superior athlete is the best way to get into college and get ahead in life. For a few chosen individuals, this is a workable path to success, but only for a few.

- Less than 1 percent of young people who participate in organized sports will ever win a college athletic scholarship.
- Ninety-eight percent of Division 1 college football players are never even drafted by a professional team.
- Only one in 4,350 high school football players is ever drafted by the pros. This averages out to about one player per year for every 100 high school football teams.

There is a real problem with the unrealistic view that being a terrific athlete is the best way to get ahead in life. It can distract you from better, more reliable, and more constructive ways for preparing for adulthood. By placing athletics above other school activities, you might not only have the disappointment of a failed dream, but also be left without the educational skills you need to succeed.

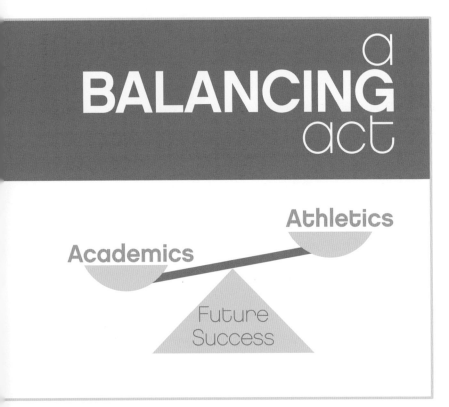

a
BALANCING
act

Athletics

Academics

Future
Success

HE'S A NATURAL

Tiger Woods started playing golf as a toddler.

Dylan Oliver got his first skateboarding sponsor at age 4.

Freddy Adu began playing major league soccer for D.C. United at age 14.

Another problem with external competition can come from parents. Fearing that their children will be left behind athletically, some parents put their kids in competitive sports at younger ages. Kids may not even get the chance to decide if they want to participate. While there is no reason why children can't become specialists in a sport even before they start elementary school, it should be their choice, not their parents'.

Highly competitive leagues and aggressive year-round play at a young age may create psychological pressure that children are just too young to handle. This situation can also be an invitation to accidental injuries. The National Safe Kids Campaign estimates that one of every three children ages 5 to 14 is injured in organized athletic competition.

HURTING
for a Win

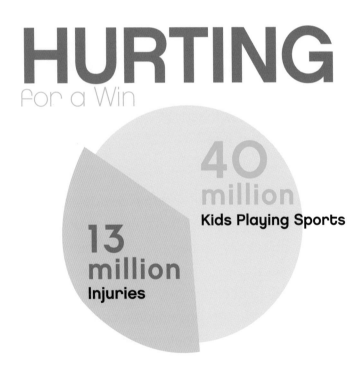

40 million
Kids Playing Sports

13 million
Injuries

Academic Competition

Competition involves more than just the body. You can also compete with your mind. Today, it seems that academic pressure begins at a younger and younger age. Wendy Soe, a high school junior, explains it this way: "High school kids are subconsciously being sent a message that says they won't have a stable financial future if they can't get into college, and to get into a good college, they have to excel at high school, and to excel at high school, they have to be better than their peers."

High school is becoming more intense. As a result of increased competition in college admissions, almost twice as many students in the United States are taking advanced placement classes in high school now than were taking them 20 years ago. This is especially true in harder classes like advanced science and math. Some students thrive on academic competition, but many are stressed-out by their heavy schedules and the pressure to do well at everything. Instead of coping with their weaknesses and building on their strengths, they turn to cheating in order to keep up.

6%

of students polled by the Josephson Institute of Ethics agreed with the statement, **"My parents would rather I cheat than get bad grades."**

Audrey Lin wanted to be **valedictorian** at competitive Mission San Jose High School in Fremont, California. She wanted it so much that she told her parents she would die if she was not the first in her class. She studied constantly, sometimes getting only three or four hours of sleep for days at a time. She gave up evening and weekend socializing to study.

In a different poll,

22%

said they had handed in homework done by a parent.

74%

of all middle and high school students said they had cheated on a test at least once within the past year.

And she cheated.

When she graduated, she achieved her goal and was class valedictorian.

Unlike many cheaters, Lin was bothered by the fact that she had copied homework and gotten advance notice of test questions from other students. A year later, she came clean in public. She admitted that she had not earned her valedictorian status and returned her award. After her confession, she received both praise for her honesty and criticism for giving her high school a bad reputation.

Cheating is not unique to Lin's school. A 2002 study by the Josephson Institute of Ethics found that 74 percent of all middle and high school students said they had cheated on a test at least once within the past year. This shows that cheating is common in both public and religious schools.

Who Cheats?

Students who cheat usually give one of the following excuses:

- not enough time to do the work
- parental pressure to get good grades
- fear that others will get ahead of them
- everyone does it, so they will be at a disadvantage if they don't
- laziness or lack of preparation

Students who do not cheat ignore cheaters rather than risk criticism from their friends for turning them in. Even teachers may avoid confronting cheating students. One study found that one-third of the teachers polled knew that a student had cheated and did nothing about it.

Cheating at Athletics

Cheating is not limited to schoolwork. The Wilcox High School football team in Santa Clara, California, was having a good season in 2003. They had won six games and tied one by the end of October. A league championship seemed to be within reach. But the team's dream of finishing at the top was destroyed when a school counselor discovered that a senior special teams player whose GPA was below the 2.0 required to participate in interscholastic sports had forged a teacher's signature on a document making him academically eligible.

The Wilcox team had to forfeit every game in which this player had played. A single player who desperately wanted to make the team had ruined the season for everyone. "My emotions took over and I pulled one of the stupidest things I could have done. . . . I tried to cheat the system," he later wrote.

Cheating in athletics happens several other ways, too. For example, it is cheating if players alter their equipment in ways that violate the rules of the sport. By far the most widespread form of athletic cheating is through the use of prohibited performance-enhancing drugs.

Highschool
123 Flanders
Farmington, MI 48335

• Academic Eligibility •

Principal Sandra Ramirez

Taking drugs to improve performance is not a new idea. A century ago, Thomas Hicks, an Olympic marathon runner, nearly died after drinking a combination of alcohol and **strychnine** (a poison) because it was supposed to make him run faster. In 1976, the Olympic Committee began testing participants for banned drugs. They have found some each time.

Still, people are trying to beat the system. Chemists try to develop drugs that will enhance players' strength and performance but be undetectable—and this has gotten athletes disqualified, and coaches arrested. What's more, drug abuse isn't limited to professionals. In 2001, the Healthy Competition Foundation estimated that about 5 percent of all 12- to 17-year-olds (approximately one million kids) had used performance-enhancing drugs.

A **Dangerous** Game

Anabolic steroids are one among the most dangerous of the illegal performance-enhancing drugs. The risks include the following side effects:

- liver damage
- kidney problems
- impaired sexual performance
- severe acne
- impaired reproductive abilities

Killing to Win

Competition brings out other forms of aggression, and sometimes it isn't in the players.

FACT: One father beat another father to death after an argument about rough play at a youth ice hockey practice in Massachusetts in 2000.

FACT: In France, Christophe Fauviau, father of 16-year-old tennis player Maxime, was charged with adding a prescription antianxiety drug to the water bottles of his son's opponents. Several players were hospitalized, and one died from falling asleep at the wheel.

FACT: Wanda Holloway of Channelview, Texas, wanted her daughter to be a cheerleader so badly that she hired someone to kill the mother of another girl who was trying out for the team in hopes that the girl would be too upset to compete. Holloway was put in jail.

- **development of female characteristics in males and male characteristics in females**
- **risk of "roid rage"—a hair-trigger temper and sudden, out-of-control bursts of anger and violence**

Time to Self-Check:
Is It All Making Sense?

Ask yourself the following questions about what you just read. Does the answer pop into your head? If not, you might want to go back and look it over one more time.

√ What are some of the negatives of competition?

√ What happens when a person takes a personal goal to extremes?

√ What do some students and parents believe about a professional sports career?

√ What may be neglected if a student focuses primarily on sports?

√ What happens to some kids who play sports too early?

√ What do many students turn to in order to keep up with everything?

√ How is cheating transferred to the world of athletics?

√ Who often has the most trouble with hostility and anger in sports?

It's the Competition

It's the competition,
And you've already won.
The competition lasts but moments,
Though the training's taken years.
It wasn't the winning alone
That was worth the work and tears.
The applause will be forgotten,
The prize will be misplaced,
But the long hard hours of practice
Will never be a waste.
For in trying to win you build a skill,
You learn that winning depends on will.
You never grow by how much you win;
You only grow by how much you put in.
So any challenge you've just begun,
Put forth your best effort.

This quote was written by William F. Halsey and is often used as inspiration for cheerleaders. It can be found at www.boardofwisdom.com/default.asp?start=11&topic= 1005&listname=competition.

chapter five

Derell, 17

make it
work for you

make it work for you

KEEPING HIS GOAL IN MIND INSPIRED DERELL TO DO HIS BEST

Keeping Competition Postive

Derell went to a high school where only a few students planned to attend a four-year college. Many graduates went straight to work or joined the military. A few went to community college. Derell was determined to be the first in his family to get a college degree. He used this goal to motivate himself to take the hardest courses available and do his best in each one of them. Because his school was not academically strong, a student did not have to work too hard to be outstanding.

Derell realized that when it came to college admissions, he would be competing not against other students from his school but against a statewide pool of applicants whose preparation might be better than his. Keeping his goal in mind inspired Derell to do his best, not just enough to get by. When he graduated, he had the choice of attending several four-year schools.

Setting Goals

Some people thrive on competition and seek it out. Others are crushed by it and withdraw. Many people compete but pay a high price in terms of stress and anxiety.

Competition can be a powerful motivator and a positive force. To benefit from it, you must be able to make choices about when and how to compete. To do that, you need to set goals and evaluate whether each competition will help you reach them or not. People who do not understand their goals may put a lot of energy into competitions that are neither healthy nor rewarding.

You need to SET GOALS and EVALUATE whether each competition will help you reach them or not.

To help you set goals, ask yourself these questions:

- What is my goal for this particular competition?
- How does it fit into my larger goals?
- Is this a team goal or my individual goal?
- Why is reaching this goal important to me?
- Do I enjoy working hard toward achieving this?
- Is the goal a worthwhile test of my abilities?
- Do I expect public recognition of my skills?
- Is this my goal or the goal of my friends, coach, or family?

The ANATOMY of an Achievable Goal

GOAL

Personally important to you

Clearly defined with specific plan of action

Reasonable chance of reaching

Within your power to achieve

Patrick loved the theater. More than anything, he wanted a part in the school musical. His singing teacher helped him prepare an audition piece that he practiced repeatedly. On the day of the audition, Patrick saw several classmates at the bus stop looking over his music.

"Look at the singing wimp," said one of them.

"Hey, Patrick, bet I can beat you to the corner and back."

"Yeah, you probably can," agreed Patrick.

"C'mon then, let's race!"

"No, thanks," Patrick replied. "You're fast and I know you can win."

Patrick was practicing being a selective competitor. He knew his goal was to win a part in the school play. He was not interested in racing because that competition had no value to him.

Once your goals are in place, you can become a selective competitor. These competitors know:

- why they are competing;
- how much effort they are willing to expend;
- whether the competition will help them improve and reach larger goals;
- that it's OK to ignore other competitions.

GOAL SETTING:
The Road to Success

Define a goal

Outline the steps

Consider possible obstacles

Set deadlines

SETTING
A GOAL

HOW COMPETITIVE ARE YOU?

Read the following questions and answer them with one of the following:

ALMOST NEVER OCCASIONALLY FREQUENTLY ALMOST ALWAYS

1. I play sports mainly to win.
2. I dislike trying new activities.
3. I would rather work on a project alone than as part of a team.
4. I think I am smarter than most of my friends.
5. Sometimes I lie to my friends about my accomplishments.
6. I would do almost anything to avoid losing.
7. I see stress as a challenge.
8. I would cheat if I thought I wouldn't get caught.
9. I get very upset when my team loses.
10. When I do well, my parents like me more than they like my siblings.
11. It is important to me that others recognize my achievements.
12. I would be satisfied if I got a personal award even if my team lost.

Scoring: Almost Never (1), Occasionally (2), Frequently (3), Almost Always (4)

12–24 Not very competitive
25–36 Average competitiveness
36 and up Highly competitive

The Parent's Part

Part of a parent's job is to help children set goals and motivate them to reach those goals. Parents want their children to succeed and often have useful experience and knowledge to share. But young people like you may have a difficult time if your parents become too involved in your competitions. You may not want to compete in areas that are important to your parents. You may feel guilty, stressed, and anxious about not being "good enough." Or you may get angry because your parents will not accept that you are already doing the best you can.

If you feel that adults in your life are asking too much of you or have set unrealistic goals for you, sit down and talk to them. They may be completely unaware of how much pressure they are putting on you, or they may feel the extra pressure is for your own good. Talking about this can be tough. Take it slow. Be patient with them and with yourself. Talk logically and not emotionally.

STEPS FOR TALKING
with Your Parents

1. **Figure out precisely what you want to change before beginning.**

2. **If possible, enlist the help of another adult (coach, relative, etc.).**

3. **Look at your schedule together and try to rearrange or lessen its demands.**

Parents often encourage their children to excel at academics. This is a a very important goal—as long as it is not carried to the extreme. Sometimes parents need to hear a realistic assessment of your strengths and weaknesses from a teacher or school counselor, so don't be afraid to get everyone together to talk things out.

Dealing with the Perfectionist in Yourself

Not all competitive pressures come from outside. Perfectionists spend hours doing homework, practicing a skill, or agonizing over what clothes to wear. They don't do this because they want to be better than their friends; they do it because they are afraid of making mistakes.

PERFECTIONISM

is not a quest for the best. It is a fixation on the worst in ourselves, the part that tells us that nothing we do will ever be good enough—that we should try again.   —Julia Cameron

Source: http://www.brainyquote.com/quotes/quotes/j/juliacamer169159.html

When perfectionists make a mistake, they are terribly hard on themselves, replaying the error in their minds and promising themselves to do better next time. Often they avoid trying new things that might be fun or interesting because of their fear of looking stupid or incompetent in front of others. Sometimes their friends think they are obnoxious because they appear fixated on their own performance and obsessed with achievement in everything they do. It is not the image they want to put forth, however.

if you are a
perfectionist

TRY TO REMEMBER THAT
NO ONE CAN BE PERFECT.
NO ONE, NOT EVEN YOUR PARENTS, EXPECTS PERFECTION FROM YOU.

Ask yourself what you really enjoy doing, and concentrate on doing that one thing well. Make yourself try something new that you may not be good at. Set a time limit on how long you will practice, do homework, or prepare for a date—and then STOP when the time is up and do something else entirely.

Perfectionism is a dangerous state of mind in an imperfect world. The best way is to forget doubts and set about the task in hand. . . . If you are doing your best, you will not have time to worry about failure.

~Robert Silliman Hillyer

Source: http://quotations.about.com/cs/
inspirationquotes/a/Goals6.htm

When or if the critical voice inside of you is not satisfied, try consciously thinking about an enjoyable experience that may not have been perfect but was still really enjoyable. You might also want to talk to a counselor about your goals and if they truly are realistic.

Living with Competition

Everyone goes through life judging themselves, judging others, and being judged. It is normal to want to know where you stand in relation to others socially, academically, athletically, and even financially.

Competition is probably always going to be part of your life. You cannot control how other people choose to compete. As Olympic skier A. J. Kitt once said, "You have no control over what the other guy does. You only have control over what you do." You can control your reactions by taking charge of your own goals. The drive to compete CAN work for you.

Everyone has a different level of comfort with competition. Look at the competitive situations you are involved in right now, at this very moment. Also give some thought to the ones you would like to get involved in somewhere down the road. Now ask yourself:

- Why are you competing? What is your true motivation?
- What will you gain from this experience? Will it help you improve skills, gain knowledge, or make new friends?
- Is the level of competition right for you?
- Can you win or lose with equal maturity and manners?

After asking yourself these important questions, if you still choose to compete, do your best and play your hardest. In the words of National Hockey League star Gordie Howe, "You find that you have peace of mind and can enjoy yourself, get more sleep, and rest when you know that it was a one-hundred-percent effort that you gave—win or lose."

Hockey legend Gordie Howe

Look back at the quiz at the beginning of the book. Read over your answers. Would you answer them differently now? Hopefully, you would get every single one of them right (even if you're not a perfectionist!). Next ask yourself these questions:

- What did I learn about competition that surprised me?
- Were there some personal stories here that I could relate to?
- Did something I read change my perspective on an element of competition?
- What did I learn about my own attitudes about competition?
- If I told a friend about this book, what would I say about it?
- How do I look at the kinds of competition I have in my life right now?

Competition involves the good, the bad, and the ugly. Look at the chart below. What did you read that you would list under each heading? Look at the examples already provided for you.

competition is . . . .

HELPFUL	HARMFUL
is motivating	**is too demanding**
teaches new skills	**can cause injury**
introduces you to new friends	**takes up a lot of time**
_____	_____
_____	_____
_____	_____
_____	

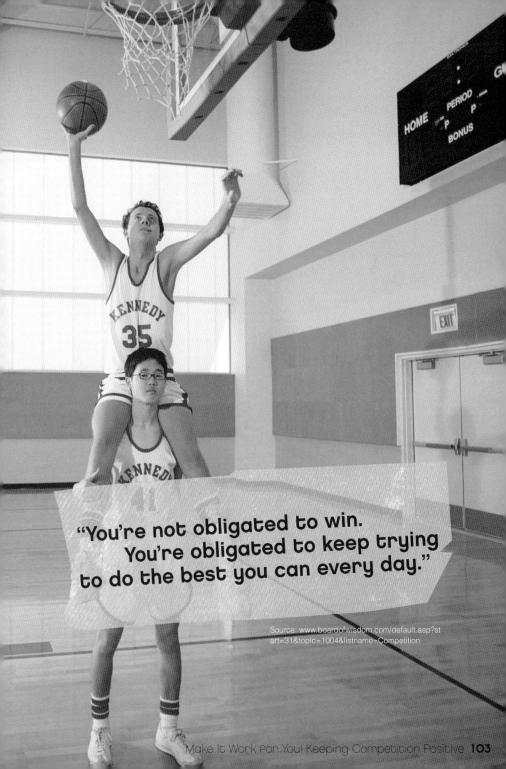

"You're not obligated to win. You're obligated to keep trying to do the best you can every day."

Source: www.boardofwisdom.com/default.asp?start=31&topic=1004&listname=Competition

anorexia nervosa—a psychological disorder in which an individual stops eating or goes on an extreme diet out of fear of being fat or gaining weight; the resulting weight loss can cause serious damage to the individual's health

clique—an exclusive social group that limits membership

external competition—competition in which the rules regulate how all individuals are to compete and usually specify that one person or group wins and everyone else loses

industrialist—an owner of manufacturing businesses

instinctively—in a naturally or genetically controlled manner

internal competition—competition in which an individual strives to meet a goal that he or she has set, rather than trying to beat other people

mononucleosis—an infectious disease that lasts several weeks to several months and causes tiredness, muscle aches, fever, and sore throat

process goals—goals that promote mastery of a skill independent of winning or losing, which build toward a greater goal

Protestant—relating to a Christian group that does not belong to the Roman Catholic or Orthodox church

strychnine—bitter poison often used to kill rats and mice; acts as a stimulant on the body

trait—characteristic that, if genetic in origin, can be passed on to the next generation

valedictorian—the individual in a graduating class with the best grades or highest grade point average

Books

Bauer, Joan. *Sticks*. New York: Delacorte, 1996.

Karnes, Frances A., and Tracey L. Riley. *Competitions for Talented Kids*. Waco, Tex.: Prufrock Press, 2005.

Walker, Stuart H. *Winning: The Psychology of Competition*. New York: W. W. Norton, 1986.

Periodicals

Ferguson, Andrew. "Inside the Crazy Culture of Kids Sports: Competitive Athletics Can Help Keep Children Happy and Out of Trouble—But It Takes Over Some Families' Lives." *Time* 154 (July 12, 1999): 36.

Koretz, Gene. "Are Women Less Competitive?" *Business Week* 3811 (December 9, 2002): 28.

Talbot, Margaret. "Girls Just Want to Be Mean." *New York Times Magazine*, February 24, 2002, p. 24.

OTHER

Miracle. Directed by Gavin O'Connor. Walt Disney Video: 2004. A docudrama about the 1980 United States ice hockey team's gold medal victory

Spellbound. Directed by Jeffrey Blitz. Sony Pictures: 2002. A documentary about the National Spelling Bee in Washington, D.C., focusing on the competition among eight participants

Online Sites & Organizations

"It's All in the Timing"
Robert Ebisch in *Sky* magazine
(December 1995), reprinted at
*www.finishlynx.com/lynx/press/
DELTAINF.pdf*

The story of the race between
Olympic swimmers Tim McKee
and Gunnar Larsson

**Healthy Competition
Organization**
PO Box 81289
Chicago, IL 60681-0289
(312) 297-5824
*http://www.healthycompetition.
org*

Information and education
about healthy competition
programs and performance-
enhancing drugs for students,
teachers, and coaches

**Josephson Institute for
Ethics**
9841 Airport Boulevard
Suite #300
Los Angeles, CA 90045
(310) 846-4800

*http://www.josephsoninstitute.
org*

Provides surveys on ethical
issues such as cheating and
information on making ethical
decisions

Mayo Clinic
"Teen Athletes and
Performance-Enhancing
Substances: What Parents Can
Do," 2004 at *www.mayoclinic.
com/health/performance-
enhancing-drugs/SM00045*

A roundup of information about
performance-enhancing drugs
used by teens

"Steroid Abuse"
at *www.steroidabuse.org*

A comprehensive site that
explains why people use
steroids and the physical and
mental health side effects

!Kung culture, 29

A

academic competition, 27, 73–76, 91
Adu, Freddy, 71
adulthood, 18, 39, 70
advanced placement classes, 73
aggression, 32, 72, 79
American Telephone and Telegraph (AT&T), 52, 53
Amish culture, 32
anabolic steroids, 78–79
"Andrea," 16
anger, 51, 79, 90, 93
animals, 27, 34
anorexia nervosa, 65
anxiety, 85, 90
athletic competition
    cheating, 68, 76–78
    as external competition, 11
    parents and, 71–72
    performance-enhancing drugs, 68, 77–78
    pressure of, 72
    professional sports, 68–69
    realities of, 68, 69, 70
    scholarships, 69
    social competition and, 17

B

"burnout," 92

C

Cameron, Julia, 94
cheating
    athletic competition and, 76–78
    Audrey Lin and, 74–75
    confrontation and, 76
    excuses for, 76
    performance-enhancing drugs, 68, 77–78
    statistics on, 68, 74, 75, 76

cliques, 16, 17
collaboration, 33, 58
comfort level, 99
communication, 58, 90, 91, 92
companies, 52–54
comparisons, 11, 36, 38
competitors, 14, 87
confidence, 46, 93
coping skills, 51
counseling, 97
critical voice, 97

D

Darwin, Charles, 34
Data, Jamison, 51
decision making, 50
"Derell," 83–84
destructive reasons, 19
Dowdeswell, Peter, 11
downtime, 93

E

El Capitan mountain, 12
"Elizabeth," 64–66
emotions, 19, 90, 92
expectations
    Amish culture, 32
    of perfection, 65, 95
    pressure from, 65
    of self, 46
    stress from, 92
external competition
    compared to internal competition, 14
    coping skills and, 51
    decision-making and, 50
    definition of, 9
    in marketplace, 52–54
    opponents and, 49
    parents and, 71
    practice partners, 49
    public recognition and, 48
    quiz, 60–61

risk-taking and, 50
self-control and, 51
social competition as, 17

F

Fauviau, Christophe, 79
Fauviau, Maxime, 79
females, 38–39, 79
friendships, 58, 63

G

gloating, 20
goals
    evaluation of, 85–86, 87, 88, 91
    external competition, 14
    internal competition, 14, 45, 46
    realism, 66, 93, 97
    selective competition and, 87
    self-knowledge and, 47
gossip, 16, 17
grades, 13, 26, 46, 64–65, 66, 74, 76
greed, 35
guilt, 90
Guinness World Records, 11

H

Halsey, William F., 81
Healthy Competition Foundation, 78
Hicks, Thomas, 78
Hillyer, Robert Silliman, 96
Holloway, Wanda, 79
homework, 74, 94, 96
Howe, Gordie, 100
Hutterian Brethren, 33

I

innovations, 52, 53, 54
instinct, 27, 28, 31
internal competition
    compared to external competition, 14
definition of, 9, 13
goals and, 13, 14, 44–45, 66
"losses" and, 46
process goals and, 13, 44–45
quiz, 60–61
realities of, 66
self-improvement and, 44–45
social competition as, 17
Inuit culture, 29
"It's the Competition" (William F. Halsey), 81

J

Jackson, Phil, 58
"Jason,", 36
"Jenn," 65–66
Josephson Institute of Ethics, 74, 75

K

Kaiser, Henry J., 23
Kitt, A. J., 98

L

Larsson, Gunnar, 10
leadership positions, 33, 38
Lepchas culture, 29
Lin, Audrey, 74–75
losing, 10, 11, 14, 36, 44, 46, 51, 99
Lotito, Michel, 11

M

males, 38–39, 79
"Marcus," 44–45
maturity, 51, 99
McKee, Tim, 10
Mission San Jose High School, 74
monopolies, 52
motivation
    competition as, 43–44, 85
    females and, 38–39, 92
    males and, 38–39
mountain climbing, 12

N

National Hockey League, 100
National Safe Kids Campaign, 72
"Nels," 43–44, 51
noncompetitive societies, 29, 31, 32, 33

O

Oliver, Dylan, 71
Olympic Committee, 78
Olympic Games (1968), 48
Olympic Games (1972), 10
Olympic Games (1980), 56

P

Paliyan culture, 29
parents, 14, 19, 69, 71, 74, 90–91, 95
"Patrick," 87
perfectionism, 94–95, 96
performance-enhancing drugs, 68, 77–78
personal competition. See internal competition.
Peterson, Alan, 11
plants, 27, 34
Platini, Michel, 55
popularity, 16, 20
Powell, Colin, 15
practice, 35, 45, 49, 96
practice partners, 49
pressure, 8, 14, 26, 65, 66, 72, 73, 74, 76, 90, 94
process goals, 13
professional sports. See athletic competition.
public recognition, 14, 19, 38, 48, 86

Q

quizzes
    competitiveness, 20–21
    external competition, 60–61
    internal competition, 60–61
    learning to compete, 40–41

R

"Reed," 43–44, 51
respect, 58, 93
reward, 14, 85, 93
risk-taking, 50, 63
Rockefeller, John D., 23
"roid rage," 79
rules, 14, 17, 63, 77
rumors, 16, 17

S

SAT tests, 67, 73
scheduling, 74, 91, 93
selective competition, 87
self-control, 51
self-esteem, 63, 66
self-identified goals, 46
self-improvement, 44–45
self-reward, 93
self-worth, 65, 66
social competition, 9, 16, 17, 18, 26, 38
Social Darwinism, 34–35
social status, 19, 38
Soe, Wendy, 73
Spencer, Herbert, 34, 35
sports. See athletic competition.
Standard Oil Company, 23
statistics
    athletic injuries, 72
    cheating, 74, 75
    performance-enhancing drug use, 78
    professional sports, 68, 69
steroids, 78–79
stress, 74, 85, 89, 90, 92, 93
survival needs, 27
"survival of the fittest," 34
"Susan," 45, 50

T

Tahitian culture, 29
team activities, 58
teamwork, 19, 38, 44, 55,
    56, 58, 59
"Terrence," 16

W

Walker, Stuart, 48
Wellman, Mark, 12
Wilcox High School, 76–77
winning, 11, 14, 36, 49, 51, 63, 68,
    99, 103
Wong, George, 25
Wood, Elijah, 9
Woods, Tiger, 71

Y

Yale University, 67
Yosemite National Park, 12

About the Author

Tish Davidson graduated from the College of William and Mary and from Dartmouth College with degrees in biology. For many years, she has written about social and medical topics. She especially enjoys making complex information understandable to young readers. Davidson lives in Fremont, California, where she raises puppies for Guide Dogs for the Blind. This is her fifth book.

Acknowledgments
I would like to thank the following people who helped make this book a reality: Dana Nelson, psychology teacher at Washington High School, and students Jamison Data, Susan Davidson, Wendy Soe, and George Wong. Thanks to Frank Baron, who read and commented on the manuscript, and to my editor, Meredith DeSousa, at Scholastic Library Publishing.